PIGGY BANKS TO
DIGITAL WALLETS

How to Make Sense of Cryptocurrencies
and Simplify Emerging Technologies to
Grow and Transfer Wealth

PIGGY BANKS TO DIGITAL WALLETS

How to Make Sense of Cryptocurrencies and Simplify Emerging Technologies to Grow and Transfer Wealth

L. GARY BOOMER AND ASHTON N. BOOMER

ethos
collective

Printed in the United States of America

Published by Igniting Souls
PO Box 43, Powell, OH 43065
IgnitingSouls.com

LCCN: 2024945847
Paperback ISBN: 978-1-63680-389-0
Hardcover ISBN: 978-1-63680-390-6
e-book ISBN: 978-1-63680-391-3

Available in paperback, hardcover, e-book, and audiobook.

Any Internet addresses (websites, blogs, etc.) and telephone numbers printed in this book are offered as a resource. They are not intended in any way to be or imply an endorsement by Igniting Souls, nor does Igniting Souls vouch for the content of these sites and numbers for the life of this book.

Some names and identifying details may have been changed to protect the privacy of individuals.

Table of Contents

Part 1: Foundation

Part 2: Revelation

Part 3: Revolution

Foreword

Most people like to think of themselves as open-minded—that is until they're invited to change their minds. The majority buy into the belief that everything we want is on the other side of discomfort, but few people are willing to give up control and learn new things.

The book you're about to read is written by two kindred spirits who walk the talk. Regardless of their different ages and backgrounds, they embody change. One grew up *without* computers. The other grew up *on* computers. One grew up with *paper* money. The other grew up with *plastic* money. Both are willing to explore a new type of currency.

Although age separates them, a commitment to grow does not. You'll find two passionate pioneers willing to think outside the *box* and outside the *bank*.

Our world is experiencing a shift. We've felt it, and we've all seen it. Gary and Ashton are willing to dive into the shift and guide us through it.

I respect that. That is why I wrote *Blockchain Life*, a book about the potential of blockchain technology. It's also why I started Instant IP™, a company leveraging blockchain technology to disrupt the way we protect intellectual property. Early adopters are already experiencing the benefits.

With *Piggy Banks to Digital Wallets*, you have the opportunity to leverage the disruption. Because you've picked up the book, you're already an early adopter. Now you have the chance to experience the benefits. Stay open-minded, and you'll see the new possibilities popping up all around.

—Dr. Kary Oberbrunner,
CEO of CEO Igniting Souls® and Instant IP™
Wall Street Journal and *USA Today* Best-Selling
author of 14 books

Inspired by Youth

When my seven-year-old grandson, Edward, saw the coin bank my parents had purchased for me six decades ago, I could see his intrigue. It's not your typical piggy bank. The metal shell looks like a book. On a shelf, it would easily blend in with the bindings of the classics. And though the bank has been around longer than many of you reading this, it's still in pristine condition thanks to my mother's great care.

Edward and I used the skeleton key to open the box-type bank and found contents even older than my childhood treasure. The buffalo nickels, Indian head coins,

and five-dollar gold pieces sparked more conversation. The commemorative coin from the Osborne County, Kansas, centennial celebration gave me an opportunity to tell Edward about his great-grandmother, Viola Boomer, the coin's designer.

Our discussion turned to things I learned about hard work, money, and spending as a boy. It reminded me how much has changed, even on the financial front, since my childhood.

I wondered how many people talk to their children and grandchildren about money and its shifting landscape. Edward's questions made me realize how desperately we need more communication and education regarding finances. Much of what parents taught my generation about money has lost relevance in the digital world, and digital currency means the younger generation has lost some appreciation for the value of a dollar.

As a CPA with a background in accounting, technology, and economics, I've always had a passion for education. The more I learn, the more I want to know and the more I have to share with others. I believe education should be a two-way street—forever learning and always teaching.

So, when I heard and read about the blockchain and, shortly thereafter, Bitcoin, I became absorbed. At first, my financial brain was a bit skeptical. I didn't understand the power of the blockchain and cryptocurrency. In fact, those weren't part of my initial project when I ran across them; however, as Dan Sullivan, co-founder of Strategic Coach® and my coach for the past thirty years would say, my interest in this technology-based system and its financial aspects became "a strategic by-product."

I could have just let the information pass by without much thought, but I understand that it isn't what you don't know that keeps you from progressing; it's what you don't know you don't know that holds you up. As I began to delve into this new world of technology-driven mining and the possibilities Web3 presented, I knew I had to go deeper. It forced me to become like a child again in my questioning—a place where learning new things and recognizing what you don't know isn't a negative. Children don't feel stupid or uneducated when they need to ask questions, and adults shouldn't either when trying to better themselves and push through to new levels.

Unfortunately, in the early blockchain days, peers and clients interested in learning more about the technology and its future impact on the accounting and financial professions were few and far between. A handful of CPAs with more of an entrepreneurial spirit became my peer community. We all agreed maximizing our learning experience meant continuing to ask questions and invest in our education. Plus, we decided to participate financially. We knew we would learn faster with money in the game. I appreciated this safe environment in which to ask questions and share insights.

A Little Backstory

Before we get too far, let me provide some personal background so you'll know where I'm coming from. Born at the end of World War II in a small rural community hospital in Portis, Kansas, I've lived through more than seven decades of technological and monetary changes. My dad was a farmer and high school teacher who continued his personal education throughout his career. And my artistic and creative mother was a great seamstress who supported the curiosity and education of me and my siblings, including my identical twin brother.

The farming community we grew up in viewed kids as an asset. They started us working at a very young age. I learned how to drive a tractor and other farm equipment earlier than most kids push a lawnmower these days. Farm kids face different kinds of challenges, but I think it may be the best educational and work environment. We learned risk management early in life—a skill transferable to nearly every occupation.

In addition to my twin brother, I have one sister and three other brothers. All six of us participated in school activities, including sports, and we each graduated from Kansas State University—most with advanced degrees. I hold a bachelor's and master's in accounting with a minor in economics, while my twin brother is a doctor of veterinary medicine.

Dad always told us our college graduation marked the beginning of our education. Little did I know how true that statement was. After graduation, I had to pass the CPA exam to acquire my permit to practice; however, this allowed me to enter the accounting profession only in the zone of incompetency. You've probably been there. It's that spot where you have all the knowledge you need but no experience. It took a few months for me to pass into the zone of competency.

Later, after adding a bit of training and some hands-on interaction with clients, I moved into a specialization in systems and technology.

Just before I entered the zone of specialization, I became a partner in a regional CPA firm. It's about this time that I identified my Unique Ability®†—my own set of natural talents and the essence of what I love to do and do best. Envision a target where the center represents your Unique Ability. Every time I work in my Unique Ability, I feel as though I hit the bull's eye. Ironically, as a CPA partner, I kept getting pulled out of my Unique Ability and specialization and into the zones of competence and incompetence. Being a historian—a person in charge of transactions and compliance—doesn't interest me. I prefer looking into the future as an advisor and consultant. As I assisted other companies, I quickly learned this misuse of talent was common practice in the accounting world as well as in other professions.

My observations brought my focus to the team approach—making business more like my athletics experiences. A Unique Ability Team with everyone doing the one or two things they do best is vital to maximizing value. Plus, this kind of teamwork allows me to work in the area of my unique abilities. For instance, writing this book has required a team with unique skills—writing, marketing, design, editing, sales, and even legal skills to protect intellectual property. And because we've pooled our talents, we can save you research and time so you can work in your Unique Ability and still pursue a meaningful conversation about blockchain and cryptocurrency.

† Unique Ability is a trademarked component of Strategic Coach.

What Motivated Piggy Banks to Digital Wallets?

As I mentioned, I have a passion for seeing what the future holds in the financial world. So, while some might think they're too old to have the crypto conversation, I found it challenging and inviting, even in my seventies. I began my dive into this new technology by investing in my own education. I subscribed to a couple of newsletters that focused on Bitcoin and later included other alternative coins. In 2017, with an initial investment of $5,000, I started the real education process by opening a Bitcoin Wallet. Back then, the transfer required patience. You had to connect to an exchange, transfer fiat money (traditional U.S. currency) from your checking account to that exchange, and then move that asset to a digital wallet. The process moves much more smoothly today. Still, most people don't have the time or the desire to learn the basics.

Since the United States has approved both Bitcoin and Ethereum (a second cryptocurrency) as ETFs (exchange-traded funds), those with brokerage accounts can even employ their advisor to make the trade for them. However, if you really want to better understand these new forms of currency, self-investing—or self-custody—is the way to go.

After my conversation with Edward, I knew grandparents needed a tool for better intergenerational communication—something that might open discussion about creating, retaining, and transferring wealth among generations. How can we use the wisdom we've acquired over the years to advise our children and grandchildren if we don't know what's going on in the basic financial realm?

I don't want this to be a technical book but rather a medium for learning. The company I founded, Boomer

Consulting, Inc., has a philosophy we employ in all our interactions. Think, Plan & Grow!® drives my team as well as my own life. My goal is to accelerate those words as they apply to blockchain technology and cryptocurrency in your family.

I'm excited to write this with my oldest grandson, Ashton N. Boomer. He'll graduate soon from Kansas State University, majoring in finance. I want you to have both outlooks—the grandfather and the grandson. Each chapter will contain questions from each of our perspectives to stimulate your thinking and enhance intergenerational communication. I think parents, as well as grandparents and grandchildren, will learn from this journey. I know I have gained a deeper understanding of the concept even as I've done more research to share this information with you.

You'll find a glossary of terms at the back of the book as well as reference materials for some of the more technical areas in the back so you can dig deeper if we've spurred something deep within you didn't know was there before. Our goal is to simplify and foster communication while preparing you for a better future.

This book is for educational purposes and not for financial advice. We encourage you to consult professional advisors as appropriate. The following table demonstrates the typical reaction and knowledge level depending on the amount of time you spend learning about the blockchain and digital assets and where your information comes from. We hope every reader achieves at least a level between Interested and Learner after you've finished this book so you can be proactive in owning your future and furthering the future of those who come after you.

Time Spent	Level Achieved	Source of Knowledge
1 hour	Skeptic	The Media
10-100 hours	Interested	Books/Podcasts
100-1000 hours	Learner	Experienced from Investing
1,000-10,000 hours	Continuous Learner	Community - Knowledge/ Wisdom
10,000+ hours	Professional	Team

PART 1
Foundation

1

Start the Conversation

We live in an era in which grandparents have more influence over their grandchildren than ever before. Almost seven million forty to eighty-year-olds live with their grandchildren, and more than one-third find themselves raising their children's children.[1]

Even among those who don't live with the youngsters, advances in medicine and increased healthy habits allow us to remain a vital part of our grandchildren's lives much longer than past generations. Digital technology, like FaceTime and Zoom, gives us the unprecedented possibility to stay connected across miles and even oceans. Despite the opportunity for connection, conversations between these generations seldom go beyond college classes and loans or what everyone's doing for the weekend.

Money lands on the side of tough discussions. We want to mind our own business and not pass judgment on the next generation's choices. That's only prudent and respectful. However, grandparents have a lifetime of experience and expertise that needs to be passed along. At the same time, we are responsible for making our opinion relevant. This means we have to keep up with what's going on in the world. Reminiscing and telling our grandchildren what the world looked like fifty years ago is important. It's good for them to understand the changes over your lifetime. Still, being able to talk about finances from today's vantage point is crucial if we want to help our children and grandchildren maneuver and succeed in the current culture.

How Did You Learn the Value of Money, Grandpa?

This is a great question for a teen to ask to begin a cross-generational conversation about money. Things have changed a good bit over the last fifty years.

As a teenager, I spent my summers driving tractors and combines, hauling hay, and moving irrigation pipes. Plus, I helped care for the animals on a daily basis. In return, I received great meals and a roof over my head, and Dad paid for the gas in my vehicle when I learned to drive. I understood very early that hard work had value and could be exchanged for things I needed.

At my dad's recommendation, I took bookkeeping and typing in high school. He convinced me typing would give me an advantage in the future, and the prospect of being in class with so many good-looking girls gave me the final push to accept his suggestion.

My visionary father saw that a career in bookkeeping and accounting would be good for me, and after six years at Kansas State University, I graduated with a master's in accounting and a minor in economics. I developed so many great relationships with people who would become CEOs and managing partners of large accounting firms, business school deans, and professors. We credit much of our success to two of our professors, Dr. Verlyn Richards and Dr. Eugene Laughlin. These two CPAs with PhDs in finance challenged us to learn all we could about the subject of finance, including banking systems and fiscal and monetary policy. Plus, each of these individuals—professors and peers—influenced my career and made me a lifelong learner.

It's this passion to continually learn that led to me sharing everything you'll find in these pages. Part of learning is imparting your knowledge to others. I want my children and grandchildren to know everything my parents taught me, all the valuable knowledge I learned in school and everything I've absorbed since. And I enjoy helping others understand the developments in the financial world, too.

Do You Know How Money Has Changed Over the Years, Grandson?

Though I knew the larger answer to this question, I had Ashton do the research. Bitcoin scares many older people because it's still in the infancy stages, but we need to remember that the US dollar, as we know it today, has only been around since 1971. That's when the government completely abandoned the gold standard, which means the value of the green paper in your pocket is no longer directly linked to how much of the precious metal is at Fort Knox.

The need for purchasing power began when humans first saw someone else had something they needed. Without any common tangible currency, they used the barter system. The value of each item was determined by how badly the other person needed it and what they were willing to trade to get it. Over time, different cultures decided various commodities had greater value and would become the standard for exchange. For a time, salt was so widely used as a commodity that the word salary came from it. Cowrie shells set the bar for thousands of years in Africa, Asia, and Oceania, and cacao beans were the prized commodity for the Aztecs and Mayans. Finally, the world came to an agreement that precious metals would make a good universal barter tool, so gold and silver became the standard currency.

In the seventh century BCE, the Lydian stater became the first metal coin. Because they carefully measured each piece prior to stamping it with a value, they alleviated the need to weigh the gold and silver for every transaction. Other countries soon followed, laying the groundwork for the coins that jingled in my pocket as a teen.

Eighteen hundred years passed before any culture adopted a printed currency after the Lydians created coins. The Yuan dynasty led the way, threatening to behead counterfeiters since this new form of money was easier to copy. Later, early colonists copied their practice to print "Death to Counterfeiters" right on the money. It may have been this danger of flooding the market with fakes that kept the rest of the world from using paper for another 300 years.

The sixteenth century ushered in banknotes. Financial institutions gave their depositors these legal pieces of paper to carry around instead of actual coins. IOUs even became a somewhat popular form of tender for a few centuries.[2] From the first traded animal skin to the current chip-embedded debit card, currency has evolved, adapted, and been readily accepted by the population.

Throughout history, the world has seen different kinds of currency come and go. As technology increased, currency changed. Archeologists love finding these artifacts because they provide an easy way to date layers in their digs.

Today, fewer and fewer carry actual bills and coins in their pockets, and checks are becoming a thing of the past. Debit cards, Apple® Pay, Google Pay™, and more have replaced these paper forms of payment. Cryptocurrencies are the next logical step in the progression. Understanding the ways currencies have evolved over the millennia, educating yourself, and talking about the different forms of buying power can help us feel more comfortable with this seemingly enigmatic payment method.

What Did Money Look Like When You Were a Teen, Grandpa?

Growing up in a rural community in the fifties and sixties, I didn't have access to a credit card or Venmo®. Cash kept me going with a little help from local store credit and checks as I got older. I remember when my dad first allowed me to stop at the Phillips 66 station and charge my gas on his account. Of course, that thirty-five cents a gallon also covered an attendant to check my oil and the air pressure in my tires and clean my windshield. Plus, I got an update on the town chatter.

During my teen years, traditional credit cards didn't exist; however, each store offered its own charge accounts. They kept detailed ledgers and incurred all the costs of collection and record keeping. Customers paid their balance at the end of every month without incurring interest.

Though my corner of the United States resisted them until much later, Frank McNamara introduced The Diners

Club® Card in 1950. The heavy cardboard card became plastic ten years later, just after American Express came on the scene. It took just one more decade for the vast array of cards we know today to begin to appear.

Like any new form of currency, many folks were like my hometown—reluctant to jump on the credit card bandwagon. Banks were afraid the endeavor wouldn't be profitable. Little did they know it would turn into the multi-billion-dollar industry it has become today.

Many think everything has increased in value over the last fifty years. The average home could be purchased for under $30,000 when my wife and I started out. The same house today will sell for well over $400,000. When we got married, a simple sedan ran about $2,000. Today, the same vehicle sells for more than $20,000. The Disney ticket that cost $20 when they opened now runs about $100.[3]

Unfortunately, it's not that the value of things has risen; it's that the buying power of the dollar has decreased. The dollar of 1972 is worth a little more than ten cents today.[4] Many variables factor into the significant changes; however, the result of the inflation makes the conversations we're suggesting even more vital.

By the time Ashton hit his teens, his spending habits had changed dramatically. Ashton was first exposed to cryptocurrency back as a freshman in high school. Because new investors flocked to see the ins and outs of this new asset class, the whole cryptocurrency market fell more than 70 percent at different times that year. Crypto analysts called it a "crypto winter." These so-called "crypto winters" have happened

throughout the lifespan of this new market. They mark periods of significant drop in investor interest and activity.

My oldest grandson discovered crypto in one of the most teenage ways possible—YouTube. After a video about Bitcoin popped up, he became intrigued by the new and upcoming technology and occasionally watched videos or read articles to learn more. He told me the more he learned, the more he found himself starting to think those people might be onto something. With little income and what he calls "even worse saving habits," it was at least another year before he considered getting some skin in the game.

At that young age, he figured investing would be something he might do after college. Like most teens, he didn't want to give up the little money he had to invest in some new asset he had just watched go through a period of over 70 percent loss. The latest video games and shoes were more attractive.

Ashton said it was my curiosity that moved him from what I call "Interested" to "Learner." During his junior year, I called him out of the blue, and we ended up talking about crypto the whole time. He didn't realize I had been following and making small investments in Bitcoin since 2013. He said my excitement for him to learn spurred him to take some of the birthday money I had sent him and make his first investment into crypto. He will tell you that simple step into risk changed everything. Now, he had something to lose, so he wanted to understand the entire landscape of crypto, blockchain, and investing.

Even as a high school student, Ashton began to see the potential of a new world. He no longer saw crypto as a short-term get-rich-quick scheme. He understood this asset would change the way currency and money flow around us. He started to see crypto as a lifelong journey of learning and investing. The two of us talked about it often. He started to follow the latest in crypto and make small investments, and I enjoyed helping and guiding him along the way. And writing this book together just furthered our journey and enhanced our relationship.

Start the Conversation in Your Family

You can use these three questions to start the money conversation with your family. If you're a parent or grandparent, consider how you will share your past when the younger generation asks. You can use my answers as a springboard. Teens and young adults can use these questions to spur the discussion.

- How did you learn the value of money?
- How has money changed over the years?
- What did money look like when you were a teen?

PART 2
Revelation

2

Blockchain and Bitcoin Basics

Ashton created an imaginary town called Digitalville. In Digitalville, people loved to trade and buy things. But they needed a currency to make their buying and selling easier. A clever inventor named Alice came up with a solution. She created the Digitalville digicoins with an ingenious way to keep track of everyone's currency.

Every Digitalville citizen's digicoins balance was kept in a magical notebook, and Alice recorded each transaction with indelible ink each time. This ensured no one could cheat or steal. And to doubly secure her currency, the young inventor gave everyone in town a copy of her notebook. With each entry, everyone's notebook automatically updated with that same indelible ink. Entries could only be added—never erased. Everyone in the village could check to make sure all the trades were fair. This made Alice's digicoins very safe to use because no one person controlled the magical book.

Soon, people in Digitalville started using digicoins for everything. They bought toys and games and even paid for their favorite snacks at the local bakery with the currency. Kids loved it because the magical notebook kept track of their video game trades and loans. They could safely share with friends without worrying about losing their favorite games.

As word spread about digicoins, other towns started using them, too. Everyone loved how safe and easy the notebook made it to trade and buy things. Better yet—the people who spent digicoins didn't need a big, fancy bank. The magical notebook took care of everything and kept everyone honest. Digicoins soon became a fun and trusted way for people around the world to do business and get what they needed. And they all lived happily ever after, trading and buying safely with their magical digicoins.

Grandpa, What Is Blockchain Technology?

Blockchain technology is the brainchild of Stuart Haber and Scott Stornetta. They envisioned a tamper-proof system for documents and secure transactions. Unfortunately, their revolutionary idea didn't gain much traction when they presented it in 1991. It wasn't until 2008, when an unknown person or group under the pseudonym of Satoshi Nakamoto published a paper introducing a currency based on blockchain technology, that people began to sit up and take notice. This anonymous report talked about Bitcoin, a never-before-heard-of money, and called it a Peer-to-Peer Cash System that would run on this mysterious web-based blockchain.

Ashton's fictional magical notebook gives us a simplified picture of blockchain technology—a digital ledger on the internet. Every time a crypto transaction occurs, it notifies every computer with this digital ledger—the blockchain.

You might wonder what makes this ledger so reliable. Cryptography is the blockchain's first line of defense. This art of encoding messages has been used for millennia. Today, it relies on complicated mathematical codes that hide information so only the intended recipient can understand it. Blockchain's code keeps it impenetrable, but its power is in its decentralization.

Traditional banks have one ledger. Though alterations can be tracked, and they generally have a trustworthy checks and balances system, these corporate entities control their own ledgers and have the ability to make changes or amend their rules at any time. The decentralized blockchain requires a majority of the validating participants on the network to agree on any proposed changes. While no one can state precisely how many computers have a connection—or node—on this ledger, we do know the number has reached into the hundreds of thousands. This means blockchain has a level of transparency that is unavailable to more traditional funding methods.

Every time someone attempts a transaction involving cryptocurrency or any digital asset recorded on the blockchain, all the validating nodes on the blockchain check with one another to be sure the trade is fair and honest. In a matter of seconds, the transaction will be verified and become a permanent record. This kind of independent security is unheard of in any other arena. Because of the enormous number of transactions recorded hourly, every ten minutes or so, the transactions are bundled, and when the bundle is full, it's closed, creating a block that is tightly linked to the block before and after it—hence, blockchain. If anyone attempts to change that block, each validating computer on the chain gets a notification, and the change is blocked, making the blockchain immutable.

There are two types of blockchain—public or permissionless and private. In the public blockchain, anyone can participate as a node, and governance is spread throughout the members. A private blockchain is limited to authorized participants. Since a small number of individuals govern them, private blockchains have less transparency than their public counterparts, which can create problems with the permanence and reliability of records. With fewer nodes validating the data, the process moves faster, but it can, at times, be more easily manipulated.

We'll focus primarily on public blockchains, which offer incentives to keep it pure. In addition to the sheer number of computers the data has to be validated through, on the Bitcoin blockchain, whoever bundles the transactions into a block and links the new block correctly to the previous one—whether it's a general member or a member with the power to validate—will receive a few crypto coins for their trouble. With so many verifications and incentives, the reliability and security of the information in the blockchain ledger are extremely high. This transparency, security, and immutability is what makes the blockchain the perfect platform for the next move in currency.

What Is Bitcoin?

Imagine that you can send money to anyone around the world with no middleman—no banks, no PayPal. You simply log on and initiate the transaction. While it sounds like a scene from a sci-fi movie, it's happening all over the world today with cryptocurrency.

Though the number of cryptocurrencies rises annually, Bitcoin remains the top choice among crypto investors. It's been around the longest—since about 2009—and tends to be the most reliable. In fact, most other cryptocurrencies build their service on Bitcoin code.

All cryptocurrency has a few things in common.

1. All are digital assets allowing people to make payments to one another.
2. All have a value equivalent to traditional currency and act as a substitute for it.
3. All are secured by cryptography, making them difficult to counterfeit or double-spend.

Additionally, most are issued by non-centralized authorities, theoretically making them immune to government manipulation.

With blockchain acting as a foundation, Bitcoin miners began to emerge. Early Bitcoin miners had powerful computers that could log in to the blockchain and complete complicated math problems to add blocks to the chain. With each created block, Bitcoin miners unlocked a few new coins—and still do.

The first block was created by the undisclosed author of the famous paper. They called it the Genesis Block and received fifty coins as a reward for its creation. For the first year, only tech enthusiasts and cryptography experts joined the mining field since Bitcoin had no real-world applications. However, the landscape changed in 2010 after programmer Laszlo Haneyczo posted on social media that he would like to purchase pizza with his Bitcoin. Someone replied to Haneyczo, who was also the first to translate Satoshi's code for use on Apple devices, and for 10,000 bitcoins, the Florida resident had two Papa John's pies delivered.

With the potential to be used as a true currency, interest rose, as did the price. When Laszlo put out his request for pizza, his 10,000 bitcoin was the equivalent of about forty U.S. dollars. By 2013, the value of that same Bitcoin was $10,000, and it's been going up ever since. Suddenly, this new currency became very attractive to investors and the media.

Why Did You Become Interested in Blockchain and Bitcoin?

Ashton shares that he was first exposed to cryptocurrency as a freshman in high school. Cryptocurrency was down more than 70 percent at some points in what crypto analysts like to call a crypto winter. Crypto winters have occurred throughout the lifespan of this new market and are periods of significant drop in investor interest and activity. So, this wasn't the ideal time to invest.

He discovered crypto in one of the most teenage ways possible—YouTube. At the time, Bitcoin and crypto weren't really on his radar. He occasionally watched videos or read articles to keep up to date but had little interest in this new technology. However, the more he learned, the more he started to think those people might be onto something. He had very little income and even worse saving habits, so he didn't put any skin in the game until 2019. He thought investing was more for graduate students who had a real job. Ashton told me he kept thinking, "Why would I give up the little money

I made to invest in this new asset that experienced a 70 percent loss? I might as well spend my money on the latest video game or shoes." Ashton says it was in 2020 when he moved from the Interested level to Learner.

I captured his curiosity when I called him out of the blue and talked about crypto the whole time. I have been following this new asset since 2013 and making small investments. My excitement must have been contagious because, after his birthday, he accepted my invitation to make his first crypto investment. Now he had skin in the game.

With something to lose, Ashton's entire perspective changed. He wanted to understand everything he could about crypto, blockchain, and investing. It finally clicked for him. Previously, he viewed crypto as a short-term get-rich scheme. After seeing the potential this coin had to change the world and the way currency and money flow around us, he realized crypto would be a lifelong journey of learning and investing. Now, he and I walk this road together to follow the latest in crypto, and Ashton makes small investments whenever he can.

As a CPA, Bitcoin as a currency piqued my interest in the blockchain. Ledgers have been a staple in the accounting profession since its inception. And, while I haven't been around that many years, I have been involved long enough to remember creating charts of accounts and journals without the aid of any computer other than a manual adding machine. In college, I learned how to create trial balances and financial statements. We also had specific means of adjusting ledgers to keep the transactions transparent.

Imagine a dusty old ledger sitting on a desk filled with rows of meticulously entered numbers—credits in one column, debits in another. These books were the lifeline of businesses. They tracked every sale, purchase, or loan—every penny was accounted for in these musty books. Bookkeepers of the early twentieth century did all the figuring in their heads. But by the time I entered graduate school, I was able to purchase one of the first fancy computation devices. And though my phone now performs all the functions I need, that Texas Instruments Business Analyst II™ still provides accurate amortization numbers and future cash flow values in addition to the basic math functions.

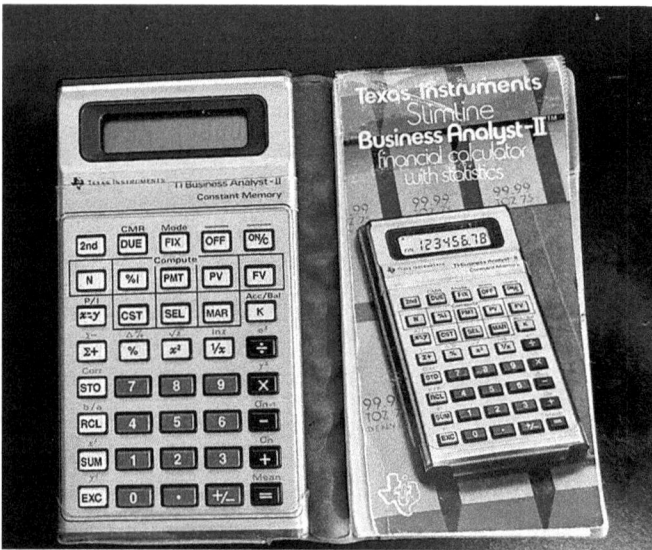

I've watched the advancements of bookkeeping with interest over the years. It's come a long way since my first personal computer in 1982. I spent hours learning the latest in spreadsheet technology. VisiCalc was first produced for the Apple II, but I was able to put it on my IBM PC—a modern computer in its day with two floppy drives. With this DOS-based program, I created tax worksheet tables to predict how much clients would owe on taxes.

I know all that sounds antiquated, but you wouldn't believe how many firms resisted this early change. Over the years, each new machine and software program disrupted the status quo. I've always chosen to embrace these changes, so blockchain technology and its relation to my ledgers drew me in.

Continue the Conversation

It will be interesting to find out how much your grandparents, parents, children, or grandchildren know about this relatively new money. As you continue the conversation, consider these questions—they'll work for any generation—and explore the activities listed below.

- What is blockchain technology?
- Have you ever used blockchain technology?
- What is Bitcoin?
- Why did you become interested in blockchain and Bitcoin?
- Explore the current value of Bitcoin and figure out how much Haneyczo's pizza would be worth today. You might use the Satoshi Calculator at Kraken.com/learn/satoshi-to-usd-converter.

3

Beyond Bitcoin

Blockchain technology has evolved dramatically since the first miners set up camp there. Within two years, programmers had taken the open-source Bitcoin code and created other cryptocurrencies, also known as altcoins. Litecoin, Ripple, and a plethora of other digital currencies landed on the blockchain with at least as many transaction speeds, governances, and reliability levels. But each new cryptographic discovery uncovered a little more of the true power of this growing technology. So, while I want to focus on Bitcoin and the financial possibilities it presents for your grandchildren, I thought I should give you a brief overview of some of the more elusive parts of this untapped part of the internet.

What Is Web 3.0?

In its fledgling stages, the internet turbo-powered the information age, and Web 2.0 ushered in worldwide socialization with MySpace, FaceBook, X, and more. In the same way, blockchain opened the door for Web 3.0—an internet of trust and value. This new technology and the many villages in the metaverse offer the potential to reshape the way businesses operate.

After blockchain technology decentralized the world of finance, programmers began to look at other ways to eliminate the middleman. Ethereum was among the first to make a radical change to the code. Not only did they create their own currency—an Ether Unit—they also opened the door to even greater peer-to-peer transactions by creating smart contracts that can automatically execute terms for fungible assets like Bitcoin and Ether Units, as well as non-fungible tokens (NFTs).

NFTs are different from cryptocurrency because they can't be bought or sold. They simply represent the assets that can be purchased on or off the blockchain. For instance, several musicians who've become disenchanted with how record labels become rich while the artist struggles and works to increase their fanbase have begun using NFTs to represent limited edition releases. Fans can purchase a portion of the rights to streaming royalties on future albums. The artist uses this money to front their album, eliminating the need for money from a big label, and each contract is represented as a token on the

blockchain. The smart contract attached to the NFT executes the appropriate payouts when the album begins to stream. Limited edition digital art, books, and music become as valuable as the Mona Lisa or a Rembrandt, and every smart contract transaction is recorded on the Ethereum Blockchain, giving it the same transparency, security, and immutability as Bitcoin with the added benefit of a binding digital agreement that benefits both parties and executes without the need for a paid middleman.

Smart contracts also launched blockchain's decentralized finance movement (DeFi). The Ethereum Blockchain created a platform for trading, lending, borrowing, and earning interest, removing centralized banking from the financial picture. Some companies have also begun to use Ethereum Blockchain for enterprise solutions. Supply chain management, identity verification, and automation of complex business processes are just a few of the benefits businesses can take advantage of with blockchain technology.

What Other Cryptocurrencies Trade on Blockchain?

In addition to Bitcoin, you'll find a number of other cryptocurrencies on the blockchain. Known as altcoins, Forbes estimates more than 22,000 forms of digital money exist.[5] Obviously, with so many to choose from, getting started in cryptocurrencies can be daunting. Bitcoin's head start in the arena has kept it at the top of the list of popular cryptocurrencies. Plus, it has a limit of twenty-one million coins built into its code, so the closer we get to that number, the more valuable the currency becomes. The Ether Unit continues to hold the second spot and has also risen in value significantly since its inception.

Litecoin, Tether, Ripple, and Solana represent only a few of the more popular digital currencies. Each has advantages and disadvantages, and values change by the second, so it's vital to do your research before you invest in cryptocurrency with less familiarity. For instance, not all cryptocurrencies are decentralized. A centralized entity controls Central Bank Digital Currencies (CBDCs), and partially decentralized crypto, like Ripple, has decentralized features and is attached to a centralized entity.

Regardless of which cryptocurrency you choose, you'll find a few universal benefits:

- Cryptocurrencies can provide services to individuals who don't have access to traditional banking services.
- The transaction fees for altcoins can be much lower than those for traditional banking, especially international transfers.
- Blockchain technology offers higher security due to its decentralized nature.

Unfortunately, there are a few drawbacks as well:

- Cryptocurrency prices can be highly volatile, so they can be risky.
- Deregulation can be a good and bad thing. Governments around the world are trying to find ways to provide regulations.
- The anonymity of blockchains makes them attractive to hackers and scammers.

How Will Blockchain Influence the Education System?

We're already beginning to see some of the ways blockchain can benefit our children and grandchildren. For instance, because of its immutable nature, diplomas, records of scholarly accomplishments, certificates, and degrees can all be contained in a token on the blockchain. With the click of a button, colleges and universities can check the grades of potential students, and employers can verify resume information. Students will never again have to contact the school to get a transcript.

There's also a myriad of possibilities for secure storage of curricula. Smart contracts could make assignments, keep track of when they were turned in, and grade them for the professors. Additionally, the probability of unaccredited institutions posing as credible schools could be eliminated because their immutable record would be stored on the blockchain. Without the validation of a majority of the blockchain nodes, the false school would be found out.

Blockchains also offer a more affordable education by reducing administrative overhead costs. More and more institutions are adopting blockchain technology every year, so this needs to become a consideration when our grandchildren begin looking for schools and continuing education.[6]

Taking the Conversation Beyond Bitcoin

Helping every generation understand blockchain and altcoins can be valuable, as can the conversations around those technologies. Use these questions to keep the discussion going and create a family of lifelong learners.

- What is Web 3.0?
- What other cryptocurrencies trade on blockchain technology?
- Spend time researching Bitcoin, Ethereum, and other cryptocurrencies to see how their value has changed over the years and discover the benefits and drawbacks of each.

- Grandparents: Explore the ways the college you graduated from is using blockchain technology. Grandchildren:
  Research the colleges you're considering to find out how
  they are using blockchain technology.

4

Change Is Hard

Only about twenty percent of the population embraces change. Fortunately, fifty percent tend to straddle the fence when those life-altering shifts start to be felt, but even these middle-of-the-road folks can't convince the remaining thirty percent there's no need to fear change. And while this may seem like a minority, it's this third that makes the most noise.[7] Any time a major fluctuation hits the horizon, this thirty percent becomes the squeaky wheel. They don't like the disruption brought on by change, and they'll proclaim every possible downside.

Blockchain, altcoins, and artificial intelligence (AI) have moved into the forefront of the disruption business, and we see them converging more and more every day. That's why it's so vital to learn as much as possible so we don't get caught up in the doomsday crowd.

Steve Jobs said, "If you are working on something exciting that you really care about, you don't have to be pushed. The vision pulls you." Fortunately, if we embrace the positives of these disruptions, we can experience this same pull. Rather than fear, we can feel a sense of adventure.

Jobs wanted to change the world. He believed it was impossible to connect the dots looking forward. Instead, you have to understand what's behind it to move forward. Hindsight, insight, and innovation take us to the next level. And whether we like it or not, failure will be part of the game. In any new endeavor, it's important to do what many entrepreneurs call "fail fast and fail forward." Many see failure as a win/lose proposition; I prefer to call it Win/Learn.

Technology and cryptocurrencies have come a long way since the introduction of Bitcoin in 2009. What started as a novel approach to digital currency has evolved into a revolutionary technology with the potential to transform numerous industries and professions as well as solve complex global challenges. As we look to the future, the applications of blockchain and cryptocurrency extend far beyond simple financial transactions. These forward-moving pieces promise to reshape how we interact with data, conduct business, and manage resources across various sectors.

I believe blockchain, cryptocurrency, and artificial intelligence will have a significant impact on my profession. I am hopeful my accounting colleagues and I are prepared. This convergence will change the landscape on every level. We will begin to look for new requirements in leadership. Educational curriculum and the way we develop talent will need to be modified. Just as the first industrial revolution moved the world away from a labor force of sheer physical strength to the world of steam engines, electricity ushered in the second industrial revolution, and computers introduced the third, the transformation of technology is recreating our list of relevant services. It's not that we'll need human interaction less; however, this new industrial revolution of intelligence means the way humans perform their jobs will look tremendously different.

The next generations of leadership will need to focus on managing the change. Over the past few decades, an emphasis on technical skills has been on the rise, but that alone won't be adequate in the future. Those with the mindset to learn and change faster than the competition will be well-positioned.

Will Cryptocurrency Replace Fiat Money?

Many today fear this mysterious new form of money. They worry that our current currency will soon disappear. Historically, every type of currency has deteriorated over time. When the world switched from gold-backed money to fiat, the deterioration escalated. Government-issued bills deflate in value with each printing. Each piece becomes less valuable as they flood the market with more paper. It's as if your mother baked a pie and cut it into five pieces. That means each person gets twenty percent of the pie. But what happens if the government comes through and reslices the pie into ten pieces? Now, your piece is only ten percent.

With the declining trust in the government, the paper dollar loses credibility as well. Additionally, faith in the Federal Reserve System (which many believe should never have been trusted in the first place) has fallen to an all-time low. As inflation increases, fewer and fewer believe in the stability of the entity.

Inflation occurs naturally but escalates when governments print and distribute extra notes. Unfortunately, this practice ultimately leads to financial collapse. Inflation rates in Zimbabwe, Venezuela, Sudan, and Argentina range from 100–600 percent annually because their governments allowed an influx of newly printed bills. Their local currency is now worthless on the global markets. It does not make economic sense to save or invest in those countries' currencies.

This isn't a new practice. The Roman elite used to melt down their coins and remint them because they didn't have to work for the money. They bolstered their lifestyles while enslaving their countrymen. Henry VIII was known as the "old copper nose" because he shaved the edges from coins, devaluing them but still calling them pounds. Printing or reminting money has always been the fastest form of debasement.

Today, instead of kings and emperors, we have central banks. In the US, we call it the Federal Reserve (aka "The Fed"). These central banks have absolute power over our money, and unfortunately, because they are run by humans who can be tempted, they suffer moral hazards.

For instance, the Federal Reserve Board and governors are appointed by Congress and the President. Though not a government agency, these positions are not voted on. Some say the chairperson of the Federal Reserve is more powerful than the president.

Though the Federal Reserve does nothing to earn any money, it holds the loan for the US Government and charges about one trillion dollars of interest on this money every year. However, when the debt comes due, The Fed never forecloses because the overseers value their positions. This bureaucracy makes Bitcoin even more attractive to those who feel as though the government is manipulating money and stealing people's time and energy.

Bitcoin's code limitations mean it won't face the demise of other currencies through the ages. It is a true separation of money and state. Though it has begun to be recognized by governments as a valid form of payment, the nations have no power to determine its value. And unlike fiat currencies, people view cryptocurrencies in a variety of ways.

Some see crypto as a new form of payment. Others look at it as a means of storing and increasing value, while those with idealistic ambitions use it as a way to protest the current financial picture. Because it takes the banking industry out of the loop, these rebels are able to send a message and still have the funds to live.

Environmentally conscious individuals use crypto and blockchain as a way to reduce the carbon footprint because Bitcoin aggressively eliminates methane emissions and makes everything it touches carbon-negative.

The thing that will ultimately drive Bitcoin is the adoption rate. Consider Confederate money after the Civil War. It lost its value immediately because it no longer had a government to give it authority—or make it fiat currency—and not one person would adopt it for general use. Similarly, as more individuals and businesses adopt the use of Bitcoin and other cryptocurrencies, we will see their value increase.

Interestingly, though cryptocurrencies are generally considered assets, some are classified as securities and others as commodities. Bitcoin, for example, is usually identified as a commodity—an asset expected to be consumed or used to create something else.

In the big financial picture, the American dollar is still the strongest currency in the world despite its devaluation, so we can assume it's not going anywhere anytime soon.

How Will Bitcoin and Altcoins Change the Future Landscape?

Blockchain, Bitcoin, and AI are bringing changes faster than we can imagine. The world shrinks daily. The communication infrastructure and social media allow us to see events on the other side of the globe in real time. Unfortunately, the financial picture hasn't morphed as quickly. The current financial system faces challenges such as slow cross-border transactions, high fees, lack of financial inclusion, and vulnerability to fraud and cyberattacks.

Blockchain and Bitcoin add the advantage of decentralized finance (DeFi). Blockchain offers peer-to-peer transactions, lending, borrowing, trading, and asset management to move from the power of the banks and brokers into the hands of individuals. Automated Market Makers (AMMs) like Uniswap enable users to trade crypto without needing a centralized exchange, and smart contracts will automatically execute the trades based on predefined agreements, giving both parties more security. Additionally, many worldwide central banks have begun to explore or develop their own digital currencies based on blockchain technology. For example, China has a digital yuan (e-CNY) in the pilot stages. The increased accessibility for those with limited banking possibilities and lower transaction fees are just a couple of the attractions. The central banks will reduce their printing costs and be able to better track money flow for enhanced anti-money laundering (AML) and counter-terrorist financing (CTF).

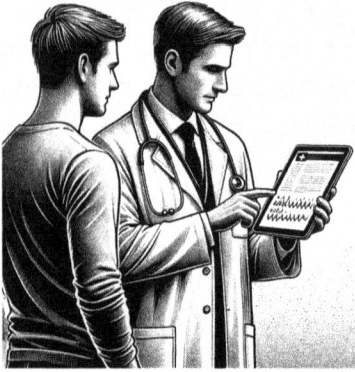

The decentralized nature of blockchain also offers solutions to the inefficiencies in the healthcare industry. It's the perfect answer to giving patients complete control of their medical records. Individuals can maintain data privacy, and medical institutions have the ability to better manage pharmaceuticals and medical equipment.

MedRec, an MIT-developed prototype, uses blockchain technology to give individuals the power to grant and revoke access to their medical records. As they change doctors or pharmacies, every bit of their medical information can follow them. Those who vacation can give hospitals across the ocean instant access to their records and remove access when they leave. No longer will the patient need to remember every medicine or the dates of their surgeries because it will all be contained in their blockchain record.

IBM and Merck have also collaborated on a blockchain-based system to track prescription drugs from production to dispensation. They believe this will improve drug safety, reduce the risk of counterfeit medicines, and make it easier to initiate recalls when necessary.

The real estate industry will see major transformations due to blockchain technology. RealT has developed a platform that tokenizes real estate. Investors can fractionalize ownership by purchasing digital tokens that each represent a piece of real property. This will increase liquidity for the market, lower barriers for those who would like to begin to invest in real estate, and create even more transparency in property ownership. Another platform, Propy, uses blockchain to facilitate end-to-end property transactions, including payments and ownership transfers. The time and cost saved by these digital transfers will be significant. Plus, the immutable transaction records will minimize the potential for fraud.

Blockchain and Bitcoin will eventually touch every industry. We've already talked about the potential blockchain brings to the music industry and education credentials. But the possibilities are endless. Supply chain managers will be able to trace products, recognize counterfeits, and predict delays. Blockchain can potentially make the transition to renewable energy more flexible and reduce energy costs. Brooklyn Microgrid already allows residents with solar panels to sell excess energy directly to their neighbors.

As these technologies converge, we can expect to see more intelligent, efficient, and user-friendly blockchain and cryptocurrency systems. But like any innovation, there will be those who want to use it for evil. As the technology matures and adoption increases, we'll have to deal with the challenges, particularly in terms of ethics, privacy, and the potential concentration of power. Regulatory hurdles, scalability issues, and the need for increased public understanding and acceptance will rise, and collaboration between technologists, industry leaders, and policymakers will be crucial in realizing the full potential of blockchain and cryptocurrency to create a more efficient, transparent, and equitable global economy.

As these technologies evolve, they will create a new paradigm for how we manage and exchange value. Additionally, when people with a vision to make the world better embrace Blockchain and work to move it forward, we'll see it empower individuals, streamline business processes, and solve some of the most pressing challenges facing our world today.

What Keeps Everything Safe on the Blockchain?

Today, valuables are protected by locks, each having a unique key. Some of these keys are physical metal implements; others contain numbers pressed on a pad. Bike locks use tumblers connected to a simple combination of single digits, and hotels pass out cards magnetically programmed to open a single door. Though the original device is as old as ancient Egypt, blockchain uses a similar yet much more sophisticated safeguard.

When we hear the word encryption, we envision fancy computers spewing out strings of numbers; however, cryptography—the art of using codes and ciphers to hide messages—is nearly as old as the first skeleton key. Every war has seen both sides use ciphers to write, send, and decode intelligence messages. Decoding games abound as the player attempts to figure out which letter represents the decoded letter in the puzzle. The only difference between these more primitive methods and Blockchain encryption is the cryptography used by modern technology requires the same technology to decode it. Every letter, symbol, or number added to the key exponentially increases its security.

For instance, if you send an encrypted message to your friend, he or she must have a key to open it. If someone attempted to hack your message before it arrived in your friend's inbox, the difficulty in discovering the key would depend on the key's length. An eight-character (or eight-bit) key means an intruder has two hundred fifty-six opportunities to try to crack the code (2^8). A 56-bit key decreases their odds of success to one in seventy-two quadrillion (2^{58}).

The fun part about all this encryption is that in today's world, messages can be privately and publicly encrypted using a key known only to you and anyone else you give that key to. If you send a message to your friend, you can privately encrypt it using your key and double encrypt it using your friend's public key. When they receive it, they can use their private key to decode the part you encrypted with their public key and then use the public key you gave them to decode what you used your private key to encrypt. This means someone attempting to intercept your message would have to try up to seventy-two quadrillion keys twice to get in.

This same high security protects your accounts on the blockchain. For instance, if you have a Bitcoin account and an Ethereum account, you'll have one 256-bit key for each account. Yes, that means someone attempting to get into your account will have one in fifteen quattuorvigintillion chances of accessing it. In case you're curious, that's a fifteen with seventy-seven zeros after it. And while there can never be a one hundred percent guarantee your account cannot be hacked, that's pretty good odds.

What Is the Dark Web?

And while we're on the subject of keeping your account safe, you might as well understand the basics of the Dark Web. Fortunately, though it can be just as chaotic and scary as a dangerous neighborhood in a big city, you can't stumble into the Dark Web as easily as you can accidentally drive onto one of those streets.

The Dark Web operates solely on cryptocurrency. It's a land where credit card and identity thieves hang out. You can't find it without a direct link because search engines don't index it. And you can't visit accidentally because you'll need a special browser specifically designed for the pandemonium.

Not everything on the Dark Web is bad or illegal. Originally created for people who needed anonymity on the internet, many individuals in countries that restrict access still use the Dark Web. Dark Web browsers simply take users through a host of proxy servers to hide the person's location. That being said, you definitely don't want to spend your Bitcoin there. Storefronts have been known to take your cryptocurrency and close up shop the same night.

Another aspect of the web that isn't indexed but should not be confused with the Dark Web is the Deep Web. Search engines don't have access to Deep Web servers because they contain medical records, banking information, and other security-guarded data. Though you don't realize it, you probably access the Deep Web on a regular basis. Every time you log into your bank account or medical portal, you enter the Deep Web.

To protect yourself and your Bitcoin from cyber pirates, you'll want to avoid clicking on email links and entering your information into unsecure websites. If someone sends a threatening email asking for cryptocurrency or traditional funds, you should contact authorities before you proceed. The good news is that as long as you stay away from a Dark Web browser, you can avoid visiting this unscrupulous section of the Internet.

Discussing the Changes, Security Challenges, and Opportunities Available with the Development of Blockchain

Talking about the way blockchain technology could poten- tially change the future can help remove fear from all generations. The more you learn about this innovation, the more you can educate those around you and create positive and helpful discussions. You can use these questions as a starting point for your conversation around change:

- Will money as we know it disappear?
- How will blockchain and Bitcoin change the future?
- How could blockchain change the security of voting in elections?
- How do you feel about AI, such as Siri or Alexa?
- How do you feel about the security of blockchain?
- What do you know about the Dark Web and the Deep Web?

5

You'll Need a New Wallet

Did you have a piggy bank when you were young? Or was your moneykeeper a bit different? Perhaps it was more like the tin hollow book my mother gave me. Even if it was simply a mug in your sock drawer, nearly everyone had that first container to hide their money away in. When we get a bit older, we get a wallet or a purse, and as we begin to earn money to put in it, our confidence increases, as does our need for maturity. The responsibility that comes with that first real wallet helps teens develop a greater understanding and appreciation of money.

That's why Ashton and I decided to start our wallets on the blockchain. We knew without skin in the game, we would never have a complete picture of this new currency. We both started small. After all, you don't ever want to risk more than you can afford to lose if you don't have a good grasp of the investment. But after a few years with my new wallet, I can safely say I encourage others interested in blockchain technology to look for the cryptocurrency that best fits their situation and dive in once they feel comfortable with this new world.

What Is a Digital Wallet?

Coca-Cola and Confinity introduced the first digital wallets in the late 1990s—most know the latter as the easy-to-use PayPal.[8] At their conception and even through the early 2020s, these online payment methods dealt strictly with fiat currency. Attached directly to bank accounts and credit cards, they gave folks instant access to their funds to make safe transactions online. Additionally, they opened the door for small businesses to take debit and credit card payments more easily.

It didn't take long for banks and major tech companies to come up with their own ways to pay digitally. After all, the fees associated with those transactions look very attractive. Still, government regulations have stopped users from loading cryptocurrencies into these wallets for many years.

Additionally, all non-blockchain-based wallets are third-party custodial wallets. In other words, they act like banks. These entities hold your money, as well as the private keys associated with them, on your behalf. This means your information is stored on this third party's secure server.

With the advancement of blockchain technology, it made sense that someone would come up with a way for users to each have their own self-custodial wallet to enable purchasing, selling, and trading. While these blockchain-based wallets don't really hold any actual currency, they are the secure place to keep the keys to your cryptocurrency and non-fungible tokens. Plus, they give you the power to interact with your smart contracts. You access these through your digital wallet when you want to buy cryptocurrency, sell a token, or perform another blockchain transaction. But instead of another entity holding your password, you have the only copy of your passkey and the answer to your recovery phase.

How Do I Set Up a Digital Wallet?

Perhaps you've already set up a PayPal, Apple Pay, or Google Pay wallet. Setting up a cryptocurrency wallet is similar. The two most common and beginner-friendly crypto wallets are Coinbase and Kraken.

Both begin by downloading apps on your mobile device and require three basic steps for setup:

1. Create Your Wallet
2. Secure Your Wallet
3. Add to Your Wallet

After you download and open the app, you'll be able to create a new wallet. Next, they'll invite you to read and accept their terms of service. I know we're all accustomed to clicking "I Accept," but don't forget that your acceptance means you agree to the terms whether you've read them or not.

To secure your wallet, you'll first create a username. Though this can be changed later, the wallet community will use this name to find you, so modifying it after you've shared it with others could cause confusion. The next step in security is backing up your wallet with a recovery phrase. Currently, this is a twelve-word phrase; however, because technology changes faster than we can print a book, this could be different when you secure your wallet. You will need to write this phrase down and store it in a memorable place. Should your device be lost or stolen, you'll be required to type in this exact phrase to recover your wallet. If you misspell a word when you type it the first time, you'll have to misspell it every time you need to use it.

We cannot stress enough the importance of knowing this phrase or having it readily available when you need it. Crypto Wallets are non-custodial. This means there isn't a large institution keeping your phrase in a virtual vault for you. You are the only entity in the world with access to this phrase—no computer or person can retrieve it for you. Your wallet's private keys are derived from your recovery phrase, so losing this phrase means losing your crypto assets.

Finally, you'll set a passcode to access the app itself. If your device supports it, you could set up biometric authentication like a fingerprint or facial recognition. If you use an alphanumeric code, make certain it is not easy to guess. Avoid your birthday, your pets' names, and any information they may be able to locate on your device—for instance, your grandchildren's names and birthdates. If you lose your device, you don't want someone else to easily access your cryptocurrency and take it before you can recover your wallet.

The Tangem Cold Wallet is another alternative. This app allows you to purchase and store your Bitcoin and Ethereum in the same application. One important thing to note about Tangem is that you have the option of attaching real-world

Tangem cards and rings to your wallet, which adds another layer of protection. You'll need to purchase these prior to opening your wallet because the sign-up process will ask you to scan them.

How Do I Put Cryptocurrency in My New Wallet?

You can open accounts at many cryptocurrency exchanges. If you have a Coinbase or Kraken wallet, either Coinbase.com or Kraken.com will be your appropriate choice. There, you can easily sign up using your email and password. Don't forget to make this a high-level mix of letters, symbols, and numbers. You'll have to verify your email and phone number before continuing.

At Kraken, you'll then be able to choose between the standard and pro versions. The standard version is beginner-friendly with an easier-to-use interface. Kraken Pro provides more advanced traders with in-depth charting and technical analysis.

Both Coinbase and Kraken will ask you to verify your identity before you continue. Like any financial institution, they are required to ask for your legal name, social security number, and date of birth. They'll often ask you to upload a copy of your government-issued identification card as proof. Next, you'll add a payment method. This might be a bank account, debit card, or wire transfer.

After the accounts are linked following the onscreen instructions, you can begin to purchase your cryptocurrency. We recommend you start with Bitcoin or Ethereum. Select your choice of cryptocurrency and enter the amount you would like to purchase. Before you click the "Buy" button, review your purchase—including the fees—and make sure the correct payment method has been selected.

Now that you've purchased your cryptocurrency, you can transfer it into your wallet. But first, you'll need your wallet address. If you purchased the crypto on Kraken, open the Kraken Wallet app; if you bought it on Coinbase, open the app for that wallet. Click on "Receive" and then select the type of crypto you purchased. The app will show your wallet address and a QR code. Copy that address.

Then, back in the app or website where you purchased your digital currency, navigate to your Portfolio page and click "Send." Enter the amount you want to put in your wallet, paste your wallet address in the appropriate field, review the details, and click confirm. You'll usually see your funds in your wallet within a few minutes, though it can take up to an hour. You can check the status in your transaction history.

Are There Fees Associated with Cryptocurrencies?

Unfortunately, we've become very accustomed to bank fees—low balance fees, transfer fees, ATM fees, use fees, and more. So, we naturally expect a fee for our cryptocurrency accounts.

Because Bitcoin, Ethereum, and altcoins are traded through exchanges, funds are needed to keep them running. Bitcoin calls them network fees, and Ethereum labels them gas fees. Most of these processing costs are baked into the transaction price, so they're highly transparent. But instead of being static and predictable like traditional bank fees, these are often dependent on the current demand on the blockchain. In May 2022, Ethereum's fee skyrocketed to an unreasonable amount when a large number of Ethereum NFTs became available. Because so many people wanted them, traffic on the blockchain became like rush hour in Atlanta.[9]

Generally, the fees associated with cryptocurrencies are minimal, even disappearing when the transaction grows large enough.

Every time you buy or sell cryptocurrencies, you create a transaction on the blockchain. Even transactions between you and your grandchildren or grandparents, though generally fee-free, are broadcasted to the network when you sign them with your private key, where miners verify your transaction and put it into an immutable record.

What Can I Do If Buying Through Coinbase and Kraken Seems Too Difficult or Time-Consuming?

For some, navigating these crypto trading sites can be overwhelming. Fortunately, after a decade of deliberations, the Securities and Exchange Commission has approved Bitcoin and Ethereum as Exchange Traded Funds (ETFs). These cryptocurrencies now trade like regular stocks. This means you can talk to your current wealth management advisor or broker and add one or both cryptocurrencies to your portfolio.

While purchasing Bitcoin through an advisor will save you time and the fees charged by the exchange partners—Coinbase.com, Kraken.com, and others—you'll need to be aware of the management fees investment firms might charge. Additionally, there are a variety of ETFs associated with these two currencies with at least as ma+ny rates of returns. The good news is that a knowledgeable advisor can help you sort out which fits your portfolio best.

Some pros of crypto ETFs include the peace of mind the regulations placed on these investments can bring. On the other hand, when you hold crypto as an ETF, you don't have as much control. If you own the cryptocurrency outright, you can buy and sell at any time. Because the ETF requires your advisor's involvement, you are limited to normal trading hours. So, holiday and midnight trades will be impossible.

The availability of crypto ETFs demonstrates the financial world's growing confidence in the currency and invites us to watch for new opportunities with this ever-evolving monetary vehicle.

Make the Conversation Real

Most people learn best by doing. You obviously never want to risk more than you can afford to lose; however, this would be a great time to meet with your child or grandchild and go through the steps together.

- Start by making sure you understand digital wallets. If not, ask more questions and research the different kinds of crypto wallets.
- Research the fees on various exchanges like Coinbase.com and Kraken.com so you'll be aware of the cost of your crypto purchase.
- Next, set up a wallet with your child or grandchild (or grandparent if you're a teen or college student).
- Purchase a small amount of Bitcoin or Ethereum and transfer it to your wallet.
- Transfer small amounts of your Bitcoin or Ethereum to each other. Hands-on experience demystifies the cryptocurrency arena.
- Schedule an appointment with your investment advisor to discuss Crypto ETFs and the value they could add to your portfolio. Be sure to take your teenage child or grandchild with you so they can ask questions as well.

6

The Global Impact

When you travel around the world, you need a couple of things—a passport and some sort of funding that will work in your destination country. Traveler cheques have been a form of international payment since 1913, and credit cards have been used worldwide since the 1950s. However, until crypto, no currency had global use.

Who Determines the Value of Money Around the World?

Each government has the power to set the value of its currency. In the United States, an autonomous organization we call the Federal Reserve controls the amount of bills and coins minted, which plays a large part in the value of our currency.

However, the buying power of each bill is also determined by supply and demand. For example, from the fifteenth to nineteenth centuries, European traders introduced glass beads to various parts of Africa. These beads, which were cheap to produce in Europe, became highly valued in many African societies. They were colorful, durable, and unlike anything locally available. They quickly became status symbols, and demand for them made their value rise significantly. In fact, they became so valuable that natives began to trade humans for slaves as a way to obtain these rare gems.

These beads demonstrate the subjective value of an item—including currency. Bitcoin only has value because people perceive its worth. Additionally, value changes as information is passed. The European beads had great value in Africa because the tribes had no knowledge of the ease with which their visitors could create the glass objects. However, as beads began to flood the continent and their availability increased, their value decreased. In contrast, Bitcoin's worth has increased as more people accept it and understand that it's limited.

As with any kind of currency, from the ancient practice of bartering to fiat money, there's the potential of using it for exploitation. Humans have abused the power of currency since the earliest times. In fact, human trafficking—i.e., selling someone into slavery—is one of the oldest kinds of financial exploitation.

Bitcoin exploitation is no different. Cyber pirates who value Bitcoin have been sending incriminating lies to victims, attempting to blackmail and collect the new currency from unsuspecting victims. But like all money throughout history, the fact evil people abuse its availability does not mean we shouldn't use it to our advantage and value it for good.

How Does Proof of Work and Proof of Stake Provide Security?

When you lock your doors at night, you protect yourself from the hoodlums within a twenty-mile radius. However, when you open a web browser, your neighborhood and the number of bad actors grow exponentially. Fortunately, blockchain technology provides a higher level of security than your deadbolt.

In addition to the high number of verifying nodes present on the blockchain, each Bitcoin is protected by proof of work (PoW). Even though we'll never be able to hold a Bitcoin in our hands, we have the assurance that it is real because in order for someone to originally own it, they had to prove to the network that they solved a puzzle that created a block. Then, these miners—people who use their own high-powered computers to gather the data and create the blocks—sell their Bitcoin to pay for the energy and hardware necessary to do the work. No Bitcoin has ever been nor ever will be issued without this proof of work. So, unlike government-issued currency, which can be printed on demand, Bitcoin—like gold—is not available without a miner.

Think of it like a game played in a small village. Imagine the chief hiding a treasure chest. He then passes a riddle among the villagers. The answer to the riddle will take them to other clues hidden throughout the village. It's not an easy puzzle, so finding the treasure will take some time.

Finally, after deciphering several clues, someone discovers the chest and brings it to the town square, where the person who found it tells everyone how they solved the riddle and exactly where they found the treasure. The other villagers confirm that the winner's answer is correct, and if they all agree, this villager gets the prize. After the winner is declared, the chief hides another treasure, passes out a new, equally difficult riddle, and a new game commences.

On the blockchain, the riddle is a complex mathematical problem. Each puzzle requires time, energy, and a computer powerful enough to do the computations. On the blockchain, the treasure is a number—the answer to the math problem. When one miner finishes the problem, the answer broadcasts their solution to the network. Just like the villagers had to confirm the winner's steps in finding the chest, the other nodes validated the work of the one who solved the problem. When the rest of the computers on the network confirm the correct answer, the miner who solved the problem receives their prize—a predetermined amount of cryptocurrency—and the blockchain sends another complicated math problem to the network.

Bitcoin blocks are mined approximately every ten minutes. Other networks on the blockchain have different time frames. But in each case, after a certain number of puzzles have been solved, the mathematical equation gets a bit more complicated.

Because proof of work requires a tremendous amount of energy and computer power, some blockchain networks have moved to a proof of stake (PoS) mining system. Some fear PoS has the potential to be less secure than PoW. Rather than validating through a complicated puzzle, which takes considerable time and energy, the miner "stakes" his or her cryptocurrency as proof that they will validate the block accurately. While this can lower fees during high volume spurts and speed up the creation of blocks because it removes the need for computation, it also opens the door for a centralized currency owned by the people who have the greatest number of crypto coins. However, the miner must still have more than fifty percent of the other nodes on the network verify their block or risk losing their entire stake as well as being blocked from using PoS in the future. Most believe the cost involved in finding and bribing that many nodes would be much greater than the amount of crypto one can win as a result of creating the block—not to mention the risk of losing the stake should anyone discover the evil deed.

What Do We Do About the Bad Actors?

Despite safeguards, every good thing ever discovered or invented has encountered bad actors. Early boat inventors simply wanted to simplify trade and make travel easier. Little did they know pirates would use the technology to become ocean scavengers.

Einstein had visions of better ways to make energy when he developed his famous theory of relativity. However, when the genius discovered the Germans were hoarding uranium and a fellow scientist had made breakthroughs with his atomic theories, he reported his suspicions to President Roosevelt that he saw an atomic bomb on the horizon.

When the team of scientists created the network of computers we now know as the internet, their goal was to empower the American military to stay ahead of its enemies. They certainly never intended to give evil individuals a world-wide stage.

Because many of these bad actors ask for crypto so they can hide their identity in the midst of their evil schemes, it's important we are aware of the dangers as we delve into this new arena of funding.

- On or off the blockchain, it's vital to maintain your encryption keys and passphrases (also known as seed words) in a secure location, preferably off your computer. Whether you write them on paper or store them on an external drive of some sort, it's best that your list of private keys is kept away from internet-connected devices.
- Stay informed regarding the latest phishing techniques. Email and social media posts are favorites of cyber pirates. They love it when we click links and enter our information without double-checking to ensure the information we're clicking or sharing is accurate.
- Consider "Cold Storage" for your crypto. Cold Storage refers to the practice of moving your currency to an offline wallet or vault.
- Use two-factor authentication for your wallets. Many digital wallets offer the option of two-factor authentication. You'll have to enter a password and a code sent to you by text; however, double security protects you from attacks.

Instruct your phone carrier to never port your number without a special code from you. And while you're at it, don't allow call forwarding for your number. Bad actors often attempt to get a new phone with your number and then automatically transfer all your data from the cloud. By requiring proof it's you, any information on your phone remains more secure. [10]

How Will Bitcoin Impact the Environment?

Most people can easily grasp the idea of Bitcoin changing the worldwide financial landscape. However, when we begin to talk about the environmental impact, the correlation becomes a bit fuzzy. Truth be told, Bitcoin miners seem to be on the cutting edge of every kind of technology.

As we mentioned, computing those complex mathematical problems requires a great deal of energy. The massive computers put a considerable drain on the power supply. At the same time, landfills in the United States are on track to become one of the largest producers of methane gas, which is detrimental to our planet. And while Bitcoin and landfills seem to land at polar opposites in any discussion, Bitcoin miners have found a way to bring the two together.

Five Bitcoin validators conducted a study on the potential of Bitcoin to reduce methane emissions by using converted landfill gas into energy to power their supercomputers. The EPA reports that one thousand landfills have or could become Landfill Gas to Energy Projects (LGTEP).[11] Though these landfills could sell the energy to any interested party, it seems these Bitcoin miners see a way to reduce their costs while helping the environment. The study estimates that a small landfill can produce ten million kilowatt-hours of energy annually. Since Bitcoin miners need approximately 1,200 kWh[12] for every transaction that occurs on the blockchain, they can easily use this resource and reduce methane emissions by more than two thousand tons. They estimate this has the potential to equal more than nine million dollars in environmental credits.[13]

Talking About the Big Picture

Understanding the larger dynamics of blockchain and how money is valued around the world can make for an interesting discussion. And you can't have this discussion without considering the security impact this worldwide network brings. Begin with these questions and build your conversation from here.

- Who determines the value of our money?
- What are proof of work and proof of stake?
- What will we do about the Bad Actors?
- Do a web search of best blockchain safety practices to discover what new technologies are available to give you worldwide security.
- Do further research on the amount of energy required to create Bitcoin and the ability of Bitcoin to reduce methane emissions.

7

Blockchain, Cryptocurrency, and the Future

F ew associate farmers with technology, economics, and risk management; however, growing up in rural Kansas taught me a great deal about all three. The agricultural industry has been embracing new technologies for centuries. From the invention of the wheel to water-powered mills, mules to steam power to air-conditioned tractors, and hand spinning and milking to the cotton gin and computerized milkers, farmers have continually used the latest inventions to increase productivity, reduce labor costs, manage the health and safety of their herds, and keep prices as low as possible to feed their communities. These men and women have made significant investments in equipment and the development of skills.

Plus, they have always maintained a curious and innovative mindset. This lifelong learning state of mind is what moves the country forward.

It's this mental drive that pushed me to learn more about the digital world and confirmed my belief that technology is deflationary. And while that sounds good, the truth is our culture is inflationary. The Federal Reserve has stated that two percent inflation a year helps stimulate the economy. Unfortunately, ever since I graduated from college, a much higher inflationary rate has been the trend. Though the United States continues to experience some of the lowest inflation rates in the world, the margin we're currently seeing is not sustainable.

How Will Cryptocurrency Influence Inflation in the Future?

According to Ray Dalio in his book *Principles for Navigating Big Debt*, policymakers have four levers they can pull to bring debt and service levels down to match income and cash flow.

1. Austerity—they could spend less
2. Restructuring debt defaults
3. Print more money or other guarantees
4. Transfer wealth from the haves to the have-nots in the form of higher taxes for the wealthy

Most policymakers around the world default to printing more money because austerity is too painful. Unfortunately, as we pointed out earlier, this devalues the currency and raises inflation levels.

New technologies like blockchain, Bitcoin, and AI have changed the game. And if we enter this new realm with a prosperity mindset—the thought that there is enough for everyone—rather than a scarcity mindset—a belief there will never be enough and a tendency to hoard—the entire world can benefit. These advancements can have a deflationary effect. And though most deflation causes unemployment and signifies an underlying economic problem, technology has the potential to balance the scales and build the economy by at least four means.

1. Increased Productivity and Efficiency – AI and other technologies enable businesses to produce more with less. Automation becomes a tool in the hands of humans as they streamline production and reduce labor and operational costs.
2. Other Cost Reduction – Many sectors feel the effects of technological savings. For instance, cloud computing has lowered IT infrastructure costs, and data analytics allows businesses to run more efficiently. These cost savings translate to lower prices or higher service quality for the same price.
3. Improved Quality and Innovation – We continue to see advancements in our smartphones and other devices. Each one leads to making life easier and better for the masses. Plus, AI's ability to personalize customer service and marketing improves efficiency and saves time and money.
4. Enhanced Competition – Technology lowers the bar for entry into the business world. The average person can easily set up a small company and compete at a fair level. This gives consumers more choices and better prices.

All this means we need to encourage policymakers to become knowledgeable about cryptocurrencies and blockchain technology. In order to create a stable economy, it's imperative to harness the power of these advancements while limiting the problems deflation can cause. Governments that develop a futuristic view will be able to support education and retraining to help people find better jobs while balancing inflation and the deflationary power of technology.

How Does Cryptocurrency Influence Future Pricing?

Because the value of Bitcoin rises daily, its buying power increases as well. Let's take an iPhone, for example. In 2010, when the value of Bitcoin began to be tracked, an iPhone sold for about $600 American dollars. Still in its earliest stages, one bitcoin was worth approximately eight cents. Purchasing an iPhone with Bitcoin that year would have been tremendously expensive—roughly ฿7,400.

Just one year later, though, the iPhone had only increased by $50. Bitcoin's value had risen to $5.27 per Bitcoin. So, in 2011, you could purchase an iPhone for about ฿123. Fast forward ten years, and we see Bitcoin reach a staggering $47,401. This means you could pick up an iPhone for less than ฿1—yes, a mere ฿.017 would score you a new device.

Since 2021, Bitcoin values have fluctuated as much as $30,000 up and down in a single year, but as I write this, they haven't gone lower than $20,000 per Bitcoin.

Other cryptocurrencies haven't had quite as much success; however, they don't have the track record either. Ethereum is predicted to rise steadily until it reaches an average value of $250,000 by 2050—not that it's expected to max out there.[14] At that rate, if you can afford to risk $50 to purchase a small fraction of an Ether Unit now, you could potentially see a

profit of $2,700 in 2050—assuming those predictors got it right. Of course, those same analysts estimate the price of Bitcoin during that same time period will increase into the millions.[15]

The potential of both makes it tempting to jump in, especially when we begin to think about what we can leave to the next generation.

How Will This Technology Influence My Legacy?

Most of the over-fifty crowd have begun to consider the power of their legacy. While we want it to be more than merely monetary, the majority would like to know they can help the next generations a bit with weddings, houses, college, or their dreams. Few recognize the beautiful legacy conversations like the ones created in this book will leave. Giving your grandchildren memories—a little piece of yourself, your time, and your thoughts—becomes a cherished gift. But if you'd like to go beyond that, it's important to know the regulations and tax laws surrounding cryptocurrencies.

Bitcoin and its counterparts are not exempt from taxes. Just like the gains you experience in the sale of stocks or real estate, you'll have to report any profit you make on your cryptocurrency. Likewise, while your digital wallet contains assets you can leave to your children and grandchildren, you need to be aware of the taxes they might be expected to pay when they collect their inheritance.

Gifts of cryptocurrency work the same way. Pay attention to the current tax-free annual and lifetime limits on gifts because that amount will also apply to digital gifts. Some who have plenty to live on currently gift a portion of their legacy to their more responsible children before their death. This saves on taxes later and gives the parents or grandparents a chance to guide or watch their descendants enjoy the finances. Conversations like those we've created in this book can provide a better understanding of whether or not your children or grandchildren will be able to responsibly handle a monetary legacy.

When you discuss cryptocurrencies with your tax advisor and wealth advisor, you'll find a variety of ways to share your blessings with future generations. Because of the ever-changing laws and the mandates that differ from state to state, be sure to consult someone who keeps up with those modifications. You might consider helping your loved ones by means of one of these plans:

- You could set up a trust. Either an irrevocable trust or a Grantor Retained Annuity Trust could be useful when transferring crypto coins.
- Create a 529 College Savings Plan. These may not accept crypto; however, you can cash in your Bitcoin and add it to this tax-advantaged education account.
- Convert your traditional IRA to a Roth IRA. These offer tax-free growth for beneficiaries.
- Consider charitable giving. Donating cryptocurrencies to a charitable organization can potentially reduce your tax burden and help avoid capital gains taxes.
- Make sure your beneficiaries know about Step Up in Basis. If your asset has risen in value since you purchased it, your beneficiaries can receive the gift at the new value so that when they sell it, they only pay capital gains on the amount the asset grew since they inherited it.

Because of the ever-evolving nature of cryptocurrency and taxes, as well as crypto's highly volatile tendencies, it's vital to make sure future generations understand the importance of finding a knowledgeable professional to answer their questions. Every country has its own tax laws, and each country views cryptocurrencies differently. Some view this money as a foreign currency, others as property, and still other countries have no set policy. You need to be completely aware of tax laws wherever you are.

Take the Conversation Into the Future

The future of blockchain and Bitcoin looks promising. Many industries are exploring how these advancements can improve their operations, from supply chain management to voting systems. Bitcoin continues to evolve, with developers working on improvements to make it more scalable and efficient. Fortunately, because it's still in its infancy, this is the best time to educate ourselves and take advantage of all the good things blockchain has to offer. Take some time to make memories with these conversation starters.

- How do you think AI, Bitcoin, and blockchain will affect inflation in the United States and around the world?
- Research predictions on the future pricing of cryptocurrencies and discover your purchasing power in five, ten, and twenty years if you buy cryptocurrency today.
- What would you do with an extra $10,000 or $100,000 if your cryptocurrency increased in value that much?
- How can cryptocurrency be implemented into your legacy?

PART 3

Revolution

8

Join the Revolution

Every new technological development has met with resistance. Henry David Thoreau warned his readers that life would never be the same if they started doing things "railroad-fashion." Because humans had never traveled faster than a horse, and boats moved approximately four to six miles an hour, many worried that a machine speeding along at a consistent thirty miles per hour would be detrimental to the health and well-being of travelers.

Even when bicycles came into vogue in the 1870s, many thought riders were foolish. And as Alexander Winton worked on one of the first gas-powered automobiles in his basement, his banker called him crazy.

Regardless of the naysayers, technology has been progressing since the beginning of time. And we can resist it, or we can follow the advice of Thomas Edison. "You must remember that every invention of this kind which is made adds to the general wealth by introducing a new system of greater economy of force. A great invention which facilitates commerce enriches a country just as much as the discovery of vast hordes of gold." [16] In fact, if we didn't know better, we might believe the great inventor was discussing Blockchain and Bitcoin.

How Can We Increase Our Knowledge of Blockchain and Bitcoin?

Increased knowledge begins by asking questions. I love to learn, and I feel fortunate to have passed that trait down to my children and grandchildren. Watching Ashton learn as he has helped me research this book has been as much of a joy as learning myself. When we realize we will never know everything and embrace the mindset of a lifelong learner, we open the door to a huge world of possibilities and adventures.

You'll find a myriad of information online regarding blockchain technology and cryptocurrency. Google, YouTube, and Perplexity.ai can be a tremendous help in finding resources with the most current information. I've tried to point out the most pertinent material and summarize as much as possible because much of what you'll find in your search includes deep technical references. If you're a 7–10 on the Kolbe Index™ Fact Finder™, you'll love the rich detail; however, if your Fact Finder number indicates you prefer your information summarized, those statistics and the tech jargon will feel overwhelming. My Kolbe numbers have validated my love of finding the facts and simplifying them as much as possible so others can understand them.

Before you embark on a crypto journey, it might be helpful to increase your knowledge about yourself. Understanding my innate strengths from the Kolbe Assessment has shown me I have a high tolerance for risk. Kolbe Corp calls it Quick Start. While someone else may have a Quick Start strength that naturally assesses risk and prefers to have only one or two ideas to work from, I enjoy brainstorming and trying new things, getting them off the ground, and then passing them off to someone with strengths that will allow them to carry the project to completion.

Learning about these traits I was born with frees me to gather information and let someone with high-level organizational skills organize it. I recognize that my Follow Thru strengths lie in being able to go with the flow. This knowledge of myself gives me permission to delve deep into new ideas and keeps me from going too far when my drive to solve problems by thinking quickly on my feet kicks in. The better we know ourselves, the better we can use our time and energy. Plus, we'll have more confidence when we begin investing in new technologies.

I also appreciate the way Strategic Coach has helped me discover my Unique Ability. Understanding what I do best and how I can be of value to those around me has empowered me to go further and have more success. Awareness of your strengths using tools like the Kolbe Index and the resources from Strategic Coach can be extremely helpful as you try to increase your knowledge of this new technology.

As I mentioned earlier, one of the most effective ways to learn is to get some skin in the game. I tend to jump into new ideas quickly and with more sense of adventure than some; however, even if you discover you need to be a bit less audacious in order to be comfortable, I encourage you to get your digital wallet and invest in a small amount of cryptocurrency if you want to exponentially increase your knowledge and understanding.

Would You Ever Consider Becoming a Miner?

Becoming a crypto coin miner is a huge undertaking. The hardware and software required to decipher the mathematical equations that gather the transactions into a block are cost-prohibitive, as is the energy required to power the machines. Though Bitcoin mining may have started on personal computers in college dorms, few Bitcoin miners working on a home computer can produce enough cryptocurrency to break even today. The only chance for these folks is a little bit of teamwork. Some crypto miners have decided to work together in pools, combining the strength of all their computers over a network to solve the complex problem. If they are successful, they split the reward based on the amount of work they did to come up with the solution. According to Zip Recruiter, if you work for a crypto mining company, you can make a low living wage mining Bitcoin.[17]

Whether you are the adventurous Lone Ranger or the Team Player, you might be interested in knowing the current rate for creating a block that falls in the 3.125 bitcoin range. So, every ten minutes, a little over three bitcoins are released. Since Bitcoin has reached values at over $95,000 per ฿1, that sounds impressive. Unfortunately, with nearly one million miners all working to solve the puzzle, your odds of finding the solution first are just a bit better than winning the lottery.

Those with a significant amount of cryptocurrency and an extra 250GB on their hard drive could become validators rather than miners. By putting up your proof of stake, you can throw your hat in to be chosen to validate blocks. Some validators have pooled their crypto to have enough to be chosen to validate. Then, they split the reward. Fortunately, the energy costs are much lower, so while you can't make a living validating at the current time, you could add a bit to your income.

Create a Game Plan

It's time to create your game plan. We don't want this book to be one you read and put on the shelf. Ashton and I want to challenge you to spell out your next steps before you close the cover. On the next page, you find a sample worksheet to use to create your own customized plan for learning about cryptocurrency and blockchain and getting on the train before it passes you by.

For each level in the Game Plan, assign a Champion. This person may not do all the work, but he or she will be accountable for making sure that section gets completed.

In the second column, we've listed some examples of goals you can set. You could also go back through the chapters of this book and include those questions and action plans that best fit your personality and strengths. In the next column, create a deadline so you and your team will get things done. Finally, add the names of the family members who will carry out the assignments and report back to the Champion.

The story of blockchain and Bitcoin is one of innovation and transformation. From its humble beginnings as an idea in a research paper to becoming a global phenomenon, blockchain technology has the potential to reshape our world. By exploring these concepts together, grandparents and grandchildren can bridge the generation gap and embark on a journey of learning and discovery. Whether you're curious about the technology behind it or the financial opportunities it presents, the world of blockchain and Bitcoin is a fascinating adventure waiting to be explored.

Sample Game Plan

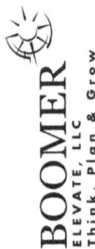

BOOMER
ELEVATE, LLC
Think, Plan & Grow

Sample Game Plan

Strategic Objective	Strategy/Initiative	Due Date	Assigned To
1. Learn the basics of blockchain technology. Champion -	1.1 Spend at least 1 hour reading or watching a podcast on the history of the blockchain. (One hour makes most people skeptical and wanting to learn more.) 1.2 Subscribe to a YouTube video like the Paul Barron Network. (10 hours provides the basics and a desire to learn more. Watch/listen to his videos while you work out. Most are 15-25 minutes.) 1.3 Write a 1,000-word article about the blockchain and its use cases. Use ChatGPT or Claude.AI to assist in the writing. (Discussing and teaching others is a two-way street where you learn and teach.)		
2. Learn about Bitcoin and its importance in an investment portfolio. Champion -	2.1 Subscribe to a YouTube channel focusing on Bitcoin & the crypto market (e.g., Paul Barron Network. 2.2 Invest a small amount in Bitcoin to start. You will learn faster with money in the game. This will require you to set up an account at an exchange (e.g., Coinbase). 2.3 Write a 1,000-word article about Bitcoin, its use cases, and your experience. Use ChatGPT or Claude.ai to assist in the writing. (Discussing and teaching others is a two-way street where you learn and teach.)		
3. Conduct meaningful family conversations about the importance of financial literacy. Champion -	3.1 Schedule a family meeting to discuss what you learned from *Piggy Banks to Digital Wallets*. 3.2 Schedule annual family meetings to discuss Bitcoin and your strategy as a portion of your investment portfolio. 3.3 Discuss charitable giving and the organizations you support.		
4. Continue to grow & protect family wealth. Champion -	4.1 Meet at least quarterly with your financial advisor(s). 4.2 Subscribe to a financial planning and cryptocurrency newsletter. 4.3 Ensure your estate plan is up to date and includes provisions regarding Bitcoin and cryptocurrency.		
5. Invest in the resources (People, Processes, & Technology) to remain future-ready. Champion -	5.1 Once you have over $1,000 invested, purchase and learn how to utilize a cold storage wallet (e.g., Ellipal Titan 2.0, Ledger Nano S Plus, Trezor One, and Trezor Model T). Self-custody is one of the distinguishing advantages of Bitcoin. 5.2 Store your seed words in a secure environment and, if appropriate, with a custodial account. 5.3 Utilize professional assistance when appropriate (e.g., legal, CPA, and financial planner).		

Glossary

Altcoin

Any cryptocurrency other than Bitcoin. Examples include Ethereum, Ripple, and Litecoin.

Bitcoin (BTC)

The first and most well-known cryptocurrency created by an anonymous person or group known as Satoshi Nakamoto. It's often referred to as digital gold.

Blockchain

A digital ledger that records all transactions made with a particular cryptocurrency. It's decentralized, meaning it's not controlled by any single entity, and each block of transactions is linked to the previous one, forming a chain.

Consensus Mechanism	The process by which transactions are verified and added to the Blockchain. Common mechanisms include Proof of Work (PoW) and Proof of Stake (PoS).
Cryptocurrency	A digital or virtual currency that uses cryptography for security. It operates independently of a central bank and can be used for online transactions.
DApp	(Decentralized Application) An application built on a decentralized network that combines smart contracts with a user-friendly interface.
Decentralization	The distribution of power and control away from a central authority. In crypto, it means no single entity controls the entire network.
DeFi	(Decentralized Finance) A movement to recreate traditional financial systems (like loans and insurance) using Blockchain technology without intermediaries like banks.
Exchange	A platform where you can buy, sell, and trade cryptocurrencies. Some popular exchanges include Coinbase, Binance, and Kraken.
Fiat Money	Government-issued currency not backed by gold or other commodities. Its authority comes from the government that issues it. Examples: U.S. Dollar, British Pound, Euro.
FOMO	(Fear of Missing Out) The anxiety that investors feel when they see others making profits in the crypto

market, leading them to buy into trends without thorough research.

Fork
A change to the Blockchain's protocol that creates a split, resulting in two separate versions of the Blockchain. There are hard forks (permanent split) and soft forks (temporary split).

FUD
(Fear, Uncertainty, and Doubt) Negative information spread intentionally or unintentionally to create fear and uncertainty in the market, often causing prices to drop.

Gas
A fee paid to miners for processing transactions on a Blockchain network, particularly on Ethereum.

HODL
A term meaning "Hold On for Dear Life" used by investors to signify holding onto their cryptocurrency investments long-term, regardless of market fluctuations.

ICO
(Initial Coin Offering) A fundraising method where new cryptocurrencies or tokens are sold to early investors in exchange for established cryptocurrencies like Bitcoin or Ethereum.

Ledger
A record of all transactions that have occurred on a Blockchain. Each node in the network maintains a copy of the ledger.

Mining
The process of validating transactions and adding them to the Blockchain. Miners use powerful computers to solve complex mathematical

	problems, earning cryptocurrency as a reward.
Node	A computer connected to the cryptocurrency network that helps validate and relay transactions. Nodes help maintain the integrity of the Blockchain.
Private Key	A secret code that allows you to access and manage your cryptocurrency. It should be kept secure, as anyone with this key can access your funds.
Public Key	A public address where others can send you cryptocurrency. It's derived from the private key but can be shared freely.
Smart Contract	A self-executing contract with the terms directly written into code. It automatically enforces and executes the terms when conditions are met without the need of a middleman.
Stablecoin	A type of cryptocurrency designed to have a stable value by being pegged to a reserve asset like the U.S. dollar. Examples include Tether (USDT) and USD Coin (USDC).
Token	A type of cryptocurrency that represents an asset or utility. Tokens are often created using existing blockchains, such as Ethereum.
Wallet	A digital tool (software or hardware) that allows you to store, send, and receive cryptocurrencies. Think of it as a wallet for your digital money.

Whale   A term for an individual or entity that holds a large amount of cryptocurrency and is capable of influencing market prices with their transactions.

Endnotes

1 Buck, Clayton, Hayward, George M., and Anderson, Lydia R. *United States Census Bureau.* "Southern States Had Higher Than Average Share of Adults Age 30 and Over Who Lived With Grandchildren in 2021" March 19, 2024. https://www.census.gov/library/stories/2024/03/grandparents-living-with-grandchildren.html#:~:text=About%206.7%20million%20people%20or,18%20in%20the%20United%20States.

2 Beattie, Andrew. *Investopedia.* "The History of Money: Bartering to Banknotes to Bitcoin." Updated June 21, 2024. https://www.investopedia.com/articles/07/roots_of_money.asp

3 Nguyen, Janet. *Marketplace.* "Money and Millennials: The Cost of Living in 2022 vs. 1972." August 17, 2022.

https://www.marketplace.org/2022/08/17/money-and-millennials-the-cost-of-living-in-2022-vs-1972/.

4 *Measuring Worth.com.* accessed July 20, 2024. https://www.measuringworth.com/calculators/uscompare/relativevalue.php

5 Hicks, Coryanne. *Forbes Advisor.* "Different Types of Cryptocurrency." Updated March 15, 2023. https://www.forbes.com/advisor/investing/cryptocurrency/different-types-of-cryptocurrencies/.

6 *Maryville University.* "How Blockchain Is Used in Education." May 13, 2021. https://online.maryville.edu/blog/blockchain-in-education/.

7 *Pritchett.* "How Much Resistance to Change Is Normal?" Accessed July 29, 2024. https://www.pritchettnet.com/how-much-resistance-to-change-is-normal-0

8 Garnett, Alice Grace. *Britannica Money.* "PayPal" Updated July 27, 2024. https://www.britannica.com/money/PayPal.

9 Bylund, Anders. *The Motley Fool.* "How Much Are Cryptocurrency Transaction Fees?" Updated February 1, 2024. https://www.fool.com/investing/stock-market/market-sectors/financials/cryptocurrency-stocks/transaction-fees/.

10 *Equity Trust.* "How to Keep Cryptocurrency Safe: Best Practices." Accessed August 5, 2024. https://www.trustetc.com/blog/keep-cryptocurrency-safe/.

11 *USEPA.* "Basic Information about Landfill Gas." Accessed August 5, 2024. https://www.epa.gov/lmop/basic-information-about-landfill-gas.

12 Tuwiner, Jordan. *BuyBitcoinWorldwide.* "61 Bitcoin Energy Consumption Statistics (2024)." September 10, 2023. https://buybitcoinworldwide.com/bitcoin-mining-statistics/.

13 Stefan. *Blocktrainer.* "New Study Confirms: Bitcoin Mining Reduces Methane Emissions." May 9, 2024.

https://www.blocktrainer.de/en/blog/new-study-confirms-bitcoin-mining-reduces-methane-emissions

14 *Changelly Blog*. "Ethereum Price Predictions." Accessed August 6, 2024. https://changelly.com/blog/ethereum-eth-price-predictions/.

15 *Changelly Blog*. "Bitcoin Price Predictions." Accessed August 6, 2024. https://changelly.com/blog/bitcoin-price-prediction/.

16 Winton, Alexander. *The Saturday Evening Post*. "Get a Horse! America's Skepticism toward the First Automobile." Originally printed on February 8, 1930, and reprinted on January 9, 2017. https://www.saturdayeveningpost.com/2017/01/get-horse-americas-skepticism-toward-first-automobiles/

17 *ZipRecruiter.com*. "Crypto Mining." Accessed August 8, 2024. https://www.ziprecruiter.com/Salaries/Crypto-Mining-Salary.

About the Authors

L. Gary Boomer is the Founder of Boomer Consulting, Inc. His current role is Visionary/Strategist, and he is recognized in the accounting profession as the leading authority on technology and firm management. He writes, speaks, and consults on business transformation, including strategic and technology planning, focusing on mindsets, skillsets, and toolsets for the future. He also strongly believes that change management and developing a training and learning culture are keys to individual and firm-wide success.

Gary is also the creator of The Boomer Technology Circles and the Boomer CIO Circle, through which he helps many of the accounting profession's top firms bridge the gap between technology and practice management. He also prepares technology professionals to sit at the management table by developing their business and IT acumen.

A prolific author, Gary has written multiple books and has been published in several online and print industry publications, including the Boomer Bulletin™, a newsletter with a worldwide circulation. For over twenty years, Gary has been named one of Accounting Today's Top 100 Most Influential People in Accounting. In 2015, he received the AICPA's Sustained Contribution Award in recognition of his contributions to the AICPA and the CPA profession through volunteer service.

Ashton N. Boomer is a sophomore at Kansas State University, pursuing a BBA degree in finance. His academic interests include corporate finance, investment analysis, and financial modeling. He is passionate about applying my knowledge and skills to creative business opportunities, internships, and entry-level jobs in finance and accounting.

As philanthropy chair of Sigma Alpha Epsilon Fraternity, Ashton has gained valuable experience and competencies in managing budgets, organizing events, leadership, and communication. He is also an active member of the Student Finance Association at Kansas State University, where he has gained extensive financial acumen and learned about the many opportunities presented in the world of finance.

THIS BOOK IS PROTECTED INTELLECTUAL PROPERTY

Instant IP ™

The author of this book values Intellectual Property and has utilized Instant IP, a groundbreaking technology. Instant IP is the patented, blockchain-based solution for Intellectual Property protection.

Blockchain is a distributed public digital record that can not be edited. Instant IP timestamps the author's ideas, creating a smart contract, thus an immutable digital asset that proves ownership and establishes a first to use / first to file event.

Protected by Instant IP ™

LEARN MORE AT INSTANTIP.TODAY

www.ingramcontent.com/pod-product-compliance
Lightning Source LLC
Chambersburg PA
CBHW060933220326
41597CB00020BA/3821